# FIFTY YEARS AGO

# Going on a trip

Karen Bryant-Mole

WAYLAND

Titles in the series
**At Home
Going on a Trip
Having Fun
In the High Street**

**All Wayland books encourage children to read and help them improve their literacy.**

 The contents page, page numbers, headings and index help locate specific pieces of information.

 The glossary reinforces alphabetic knowledge and extends vocabulary.

 The further information section suggests other books dealing with the same subject.

 Find out more about how this book is specifically relevant to the National Literacy Strategy on page 31.

Editor: Kim Protheroe
Consultant: Norah Granger
Cover design: White Design
Inside design: Michael Leaman
Picture glossary illustrator: John Yates
Photo stylist: Gina Brown
Production controller: Carol Titchener

First published in 1999 by
Wayland Publishers Limited,
61 Western Road, Hove,
East Sussex BN3 1JD

© Copyright 1999 Wayland Publishers Limited

Typeset in England by Michael Leaman
    Design Partnership
Printed and bound in Italy by L.G. Canale
    & C.S.p.A, Turin

British Library in Cataloguing Data
Bryant-Mole, Karen
    Going on a Trip. – (Fifty years ago)
    1. Transportation – History – Juvenile literature
    I. Title 388'. 09.

ISBN 0 7502 2305 7

Picture acknowledgements
The publishers would like to thank the following for allowing their pictures to be used in this book: Quadrant Cover; Ffotograff/Pat Aithie Cover inset; Topham Picturepoint 9, 21, 23, 25, 27; Popperfoto 5, 15, 17; Hulton Getty 7, 11, 13, 19; Pictor Unifoto 12; Chapel Studios/Patrick Cockell 14; Impact/Simon Shepheard 20. All other pictures by Ffotograff/Pat Aithie.

# CONTENTS

| | |
|---|---|
| Bus | 4 |
| Train | 6 |
| Car | 8 |
| Coach | 10 |
| Plane | 12 |
| Ship | 14 |
| Bike | 16 |
| Motorbike | 18 |
| Tram | 20 |
| Caravan | 22 |
| By Horse | 24 |
| On Foot | 26 |
| Notes for parents and teachers | 28 |
| About the photographs | 28 |
| Glossary | 30 |
| Further information, including literacy information | 31 |
| Index | 32 |

In this book we are introduced to the Chapman family. We will meet Mr and Mrs Chapman, their children Sam and Kate, and Sam and Kate's grandparents Maggie and Bert. We will also meet Mrs Chapman's brother. Compare going on a trip today with going on a trip fifty years ago.

# BUS

# Sam and Kate are catching the bus into town with their mum.

Mrs Chapman pays the driver as she gets on to the bus. When all the passengers have got on the bus and have paid for their tickets, the driver goes on to the next stop.

# FIFTY YEARS AGO

## The passengers on this bus paid a bus conductor.

Fifty years ago, bus travel was one of the most popular methods of transport. Buses were cheap and easy to use. Buses ran from early in the morning until late into the night.

### I remember...

Maggie Chapman is Sam and Kate's gran. She used to catch the bus to school. 'When the bus was at a bus stop, the conductor rang a bell to let the driver know it was safe to start off again. Conductors had ticket machines strapped in front of their uniforms. They turned a handle on the side to print out the ticket.'

# TRAIN

## Mr Chapman goes to work by train.

Every morning and evening, thousands of people catch trains to and from work. People who travel to work by train are known as commuters. Train operators have to make sure that people can travel quickly and safely.

# FIFTY YEARS AGO

## This station porter loaded luggage on to the train for the passengers.

Train signals, like those above the porter, were controlled by men working in signal boxes by the side of the railway track. Today, signals are controlled by computers.

### I remember...

Bert Chapman is Sam and Kate's grandpa. He used to live near a railway line. 'Of course, when I was a boy, most trains were steam trains. It was hot, dirty work keeping that coal fire going, so that the water could be heated to make steam. Mind you, there was nothing to beat the sight of a steam train puffing its way along the track.'

# CAR

# Mrs Chapman is filling her car with fuel at a petrol station.

Mrs Chapman's car takes unleaded petrol. Unleaded petrol does not pollute the air as much as leaded petrol. The Chapmans use their car to travel wherever they want, whenever they want.

# FIFTY YEARS AGO

## This car was filled with fuel by a petrol pump attendant.

The Second World War had ended in 1945 but many goods, including petrol, were still in short supply. People were only allowed to buy a certain amount of petrol. This was called rationing.

### I remember...

Maggie Chapman's dad had a car. 'We were the first people in our street to have a car. Mind you, petrol rationing meant that we couldn't use it very often. Some people could get more petrol than others. My friend Jane's dad was a doctor, so he was allowed extra.'

# COACH

## Mr and Mrs Chapman are going to the theatre by coach.

Mr and Mrs Chapman belong to a local drama group. They are all going to see a play in London. The coach they are travelling in is very comfortable. It is air-conditioned and even has a toilet.

# FIFTY YEARS AGO

## These women were on a coach tour.

Day trips and holidays by coach were very popular fifty years ago. Few families owned cars, so coaches were a good way of travelling long distances.

### I remember...

Bert Chapman remembers going on a coach trip with his mum. 'We went to the seaside on a Sunday School outing. It was really sunny and the coach was hot and stuffy. I wanted to go to the loo but my mum told me I'd have to wait until we got there. It was rather an uncomfortable journey!'

# PLANE

## Mr Chapman's sister is flying over from America to see the family.

Mr Chapman's sister lives in America. Air travel is now so quick and easy, that she flies over to see the Chapmans at least once a year. Sam and Kate have been to America twice. They have also flown to Spain and Greece for holidays.

# FIFTY YEARS AGO

## These passengers were getting on a plane to Belgium.

Fifty years ago, people were beginning to make plane journeys for business and for pleasure. Before the Second World War, few people had ever travelled by plane.

### I remember...

One of Bert Chapman's friends had an uncle who flew to Canada. 'I had some relatives who had flown in planes during the war but no one I knew had ever flown as far as Canada. In those days, you really had to be quite well off to travel by plane.'

# SHIP

## The Chapmans are waiting to get on the ferry to France.

Once or twice a year, the Chapmans go on a day trip to France. There is just enough time to sail across, have lunch in France, do some shopping and catch the ferry back again.

# FIFTY YEARS AGO

## This enormous liner carried passengers to America.

Many of the liners that travelled to America carried more than a thousand passengers. Most of the liners carried goods as well as passengers. It was too expensive to send goods by air.

### I remember...

Maggie Chapman's auntie married an American soldier who she had met during the Second World War. 'They decided to set up home in America. I remember going to the port to see them off. It was incredible. There were thousands of people there, some of them smiling, some of them crying because they didn't know when they would meet up again.'

# BIKE

## Kate and her dad like riding their bikes in the countryside.

Mr Chapman and Kate do not like riding in the town because there is too much traffic. Their bikes have lots of gears. This makes it easier to ride up and down hills.

# FIFTY YEARS AGO

## Cycling was a cheap and easy way to travel.

Fifty years ago, bikes were used to travel to work, to the shops, to friends' houses and on outings. Today, most people wear cycle helmets but in those days they were almost unheard of.

### I remember...

Maggie Chapman's brother got a bike for his birthday. 'The day he got it, he told mum he was just going to try it out. He cycled all the way to the next town! It was nearly dark by the time he got back. He got told off by our mum. The next day he could hardly walk, his legs ached so much.'

# MOTORBIKE

Mrs Chapman's brother has a motorbike.

Mrs Chapman's brother lives in a flat in the middle of a busy town. He thinks a motorbike is better than a car because he doesn't get held up in traffic jams on his way to work.

# FIFTY YEARS AGO

## These women wore goggles over their eyes when they travelled fast.

Motorbikes were popular with women as well as with men. Today you have to wear a crash helmet if you want to ride a motorbike but you didn't have to fifty years ago.

### I remember...

Bert Chapman loved motorbikes when he was a boy. 'Britain produced some of the best motorbikes in the world back in those days. Nortons, Triumphs ... they were great machines.'

# TRAM

## Mrs Chapman's mum lives in a town where there are trams.

Trams are a very clean method of transport. They run on electricity and so they don't pollute the air. More and more town planners are thinking about using trams.

# FIFTY YEARS AGO

## Many towns had trams fifty years ago.

Trams ran along rails. Some towns had trolley-buses. They used overhead electricity cables, like trams, but didn't have to travel along rails.

### I remember...

Bert Chapman used to catch the tram into town. 'The trams had these seats that you could flip over, so that they faced the opposite direction. That was because trams couldn't turn round. Instead, there was a driver's place at either end. When the tram got to the end of the line, the driver walked to the other end of the tram, flipping over the seats as he went.'

# CARAVAN

The Chapmans have hired this van for two weeks.

This is a special sort of caravan, called a camper van. Inside there are seats and tables, beds, a toilet and shower, and a little kitchen.

# FIFTY YEARS AGO

## This caravan was towed behind a car.

Once petrol rationing ended, caravan holidays became very popular. Towns were often smoky and dirty. People enjoyed being able to breathe the fresh country air.

### I remember...

Maggie Chapman remembers going on a caravan holiday with a friend and her family. 'It took a long time to get to the caravan site because we had to drive so slowly. There were lots of other children on the camp site. We all made dens in the woods nearby. It was a lovely holiday.'

# BY HORSE

## Kate enjoys pony-trekking.

Today, people who make journeys by horse usually do so for fun. Horses that are ridden on roads have to get used to the noise and speed of other traffic. Horse riders always wear riding hats to protect their heads in case of a fall.

# FIFTY YEARS AGO

## These men travelled on a cart pulled by horses.

Fifty years ago, horses and carts were still being used to deliver some goods. People usually travelled in cars or buses but there were still a few who preferred to travel in horse-drawn carriages or traps.

### I remember...

Maggie Chapman remembers seeing horses and carts. 'Our milk was delivered on a horse-drawn cart. The milkman walked along beside his horse. That horse was so good and patient. The coal was delivered on a horse-drawn cart, too. I can remember the coalman. His skin and clothes were always black with coal dust.'

# ON FOOT

## The Chapmans like walking in the forest.

Most of the Chapmans' journeys are made in vehicles. The only time they travel on foot for long distances is when they go for walks in the countryside. Even then, they use the car to get there!

# FIFTY YEARS AGO

## It took these children half an hour to walk to school every morning.

Fifty years ago, walking was part of everyday life. Many people walked to work, or to the shops or to school. Today, most people just get into cars that are parked outside their houses.

### I remember...

Bert Chapman's mum always walked him and his sister to school when they were little. 'She took us to school in the mornings and then she met us at lunch time and we walked home for lunch. We walked back to school after lunch and walked home again at the end of the day. It was a lot of walking for my poor mum!'

# NOTES FOR PARENTS

**This book is designed to be used on many different levels.**

The words in bold provide a simple, core text. The rest of the text provides greater detail, more background information and some personal reminiscences. Competent readers will be able to tackle the entire text themselves. Younger readers could share the reading of the text with an adult. Non-readers will benefit from hearing the text read aloud to them.

All children will enjoy comparing and contrasting the main pictures on each double-page spread. Every picture is a rich resource with much that can be observed and discussed. Ideas for discussion points and questions to ask about each photograph can be found below.

Children are likely to have relatives who will have clear memories of everyday life fifty years ago. There is nothing that brings history to life more vividly than personal recollections. If these memories can be supported by photographs or other artefacts, such as bus tickets or train timetables, then the experience is made all the more 'real' to a child.

This particular book is about travel. Fifty years ago, there were far fewer cars on the roads than there are today. Children could think about how this affected everyday life. They could consider the similarities and differences between travel today and fifty years ago. In many instances, the types of transport, such as trains and planes, have remained the same, but the level of services offered, the design of the vehicles and the numbers of people using the different methods of transport have changed significantly.

## About the Photographs

**Bus p 5**

*Questions to ask:*
Can you describe the bus conductor's uniform?
Look at the other bus. Can you see where the driver sat?

*Points to explore:*
Find out about the buses that ran in your local area fifty years ago.
Compare the service then with the service now.

**Train p 7**

*Questions to ask:*
What is the porter pushing?
How many people are getting on to the train?

*Points to explore:*
Find out what happened to the four big railway companies in 1948. Find out what happened to many country railway lines during the 1960s.

**Car p 9**

*Questions to ask:*
How many petrol pumps can you see?
Which brands of petrol can still be bought today?

*Points to explore:*
Find out about the history of motoring organizations such as the AA or the RAC.
Think about the extra features that many cars have today compared with fifty years ago.

**Coach p 11**

*Questions to ask:*
How would you describe the shape of this coach?
What are most of the women wearing on their heads?

*Points to explore:*
Find out about some of the seaside resorts that were popular destinations for coach trips, e.g. Skegness and Blackpool.
Ask friends and relatives whether they have any memories of coach trips.

# AND TEACHERS

**Plane p 13**

*Questions to ask:*
What shape are the windows on this plane?
What do you think the name of the airline was?

*Points to explore:*
Compare the design of aircraft fifty years ago with the design of today's planes. Talk about the reasons why many more people now travel by plane than fifty years ago.

**Ship p 15**

*Questions to ask:*
How many lifeboats can you see on the liner? What are the small round windows along the side of the ship called?

*Points to explore:*
Find out about emigration to countries such as Australia, the USA and Canada. Find out about immigration from countries such as Jamaica and Pakistan.

**Bike p 17**

*Questions to ask:*
What do you notice about the ages of the cyclists?
What do some bikes have for the cyclists' belongings?

*Points to explore:*
Find out more about Cycle Clubs and the sorts of activities they used to arrange. Think about the differences between bikes today and bikes fifty years ago.

**Motorbike p19**

*Questions to ask:*
Can you describe what the women are wearing?
What differences are there between motorbikes fifty years ago and today?

*Points to explore:*
Find out about sidecars, which were attached to motorbikes. Talk about motorbike safety and how motorcyclists protect their bodies.

**Tram p 21**

*Questions to ask:*
How many floors, or decks, did this tram have?
Would you expect to see more or fewer cars in this high street today?

*Points to explore:*
Ask friends and relations whether they can remember travelling in trams or trolley buses.
Find out whether any of the towns in your local area are thinking about reintroducing trams.

**Caravan p 23**

*Questions to ask:*
What are the children in this photograph doing?
Do they look as though they are enjoying themselves?

*Points to explore:*
Find out how they used to wash and cook in caravans fifty years ago. Find out about people who may have lived in caravans all year round.

**By Horse p 25**

*Questions to ask:*
How many horses were being used to pull this cart?
What can you see on the cart?

*Points to explore:*
Ask friends and relatives whether they can remember traders using a horse and cart. Talk about why horses have become a less popular method of transport.

**On Foot p 27**

*Questions to ask:*
How many children can you see?
What are they doing that would be very dangerous today?

*Points to explore:*
Find out how your friends and relatives travelled to school. Talk about why more people travelled on foot fifty years ago than today.

# GLOSSARY

 **bus conductor** Someone who looked after passengers on a bus. He or she collected money and gave out tickets.

 **station porter** A man who carried luggage, parcels and supplies at a railway station.

 **coalman** Someone who delivered coal to people's houses. The coal was often carried on horse-drawn carts.

 **steam train** Trains that were powered by a coal fire in the engine.

 **port** Journeys by sea usually begin and end at a port.

 **ticket machine** Old-fashioned bus conductors' ticket machines had a handle on the side. When the handle was turned, a printed ticket came out.

 **ration book** Ration books were full of coupons, a bit like stamps. You gave them to the shopkeeper when you bought something that was in short supply.

 **trap** A light cart with two wheels. It was pulled by a horse or pony.

 **signal box** A small building by the side of the railway track. The train signals were operated by men in the box pulling levers.

 **trolley bus** Trolley buses looked like ordinary buses, but they had metal cables on top which hooked up to overhead electricity wires.

# FURTHER INFORMATION

## Books to read

*In the Street* by K. Bryant-Mole (Wayland, 1994)

*Journeys discovered through History* by K. Bryant-Mole (A & C Black, 1997)

*People on the Move* by K. Bryant-Mole (Wayland, 1996)

*Travelling* by G. Tanner and T. Wood (A & C Black, 1992)

*Transport* by J. Shuter (Heinemann, 1999)

*Travelling in Grandma's Day* by F Gardner (Evans, 1997)

**Use this book for teaching literacy**

This book can help you in the literacy hour in the following ways:

- ✓ By extending the skills of reading non-fiction. There are two levels of text given, a simple version and a more advanced level.
- ✓ By encouraging children to articulate and then try to answer questions provoked by the pictures.
- ✓ They can be encouraged to ask relatives about their lives as children and learn about history through personal experiences.
- ✓ They can write stories about what their lives would have been like fifty years ago.

# INDEX

**Aa**

**Bb** bikes 16, 17
buses 4, 5
bus conductors 5

**Cc** camper vans 22
caravans 22, 23
carriages 25
cars 8, 9, 11, 18, 23, 26, 27
carts 25
coaches 10, 11
commuters 6
cycling 16, 17

**Dd** day trips 11, 14
drivers 4, 21

**Ee** electricity 20, 21

**Ff** ferries 14

**Gg**

**Hh** hats 24
helmets 17, 19
holidays 11, 12, 23
horses 24, 25

**Ii**

**Jj**

**Kk**

**Ll** liners 15
luggage 7

**Mm** motorbikes 18, 19

**Nn**

**Oo** outings 11, 17

**Pp** passengers 4, 5, 7, 13, 15
petrol 8, 9, 23

**Qq**

**Rr** rationing 9, 23

**Ss** Second World War 9, 13, 15
school 5, 27
ships 14, 15
shopping 14, 17, 27
signal boxes 7
station porters 7
steam trains 7

**Tt** traffic 16, 18, 24
trains 6, 7
trams 20, 21
traps 25
trolley-buses 21

**Uu**

**Vv**

**Ww** walking 26, 27
work 6, 13, 17, 18, 27

**Xx**

**Yy**

**Zz**